For Rosy

without whom this book would never have been possible, and whose constant friendship is invaluable

At North-Gate and South-Gate too
St Michael guards the way,
While o'er the East and o'er the West
St Peter holds his sway
Anon

CITY WALL WALKS

Stage 1: St Michael at the Northgate to Catte Street 20

Stage 2: Catte Street to New College 42

Stage 3: New College to St Edmund Hall 56

Stage 4: St Edmund Hall to Merton College 64

Stage 5: Merton College to Christ Church 72

Stage 6: Christ Church to Oxford Castle 80

Stage 7: Oxford Castle to St Michael in the Northgate 94

DEFINITIONS

Bastion: one of a series of semi-circular projections from the city wall, originally the same height as the wall

City ditch: this was usually a moated ditch, before being used as the city rubbish dump and prior to be infilled at a later date

City walls: early defences or fortifications

Encaenia: the conferring of Honorary Academic Degrees by Oxford University

Palisade: a fence of stakes forming an enclosure or defence around a compound

Rampart: wall of stone surrounding a castle or fortified city

OXFORD'S HIDDEN WALLS

INTRODUCTION

This pocket-sized book has been devised as a series of walks, or stages, around the city walls of Oxford.

It does not take long to complete each stage. The wall is easily identifiable with the use of photographs and illustrations, which have been included to help you to find your bearings. A diagramatic map, with directional arrows, has been drawn on the guiding pages to assist you.

Throughout the book, references are made to early maps of the city and these cover the period from c.1250 to 1675. Each stage begins with one of these maps. Apart from the 1250 plan, note that the compass point of 'North' is at the *bottom* of each of these maps. It has not been possible to revert them to today's norm, as the buildings would then be upside down.

The earliest of these shows a plan of Oxford as a walled town in c. 1250. A map drawn by Ralph Agas dated 1578 (pp.8 and 9), shows Oxford from a bird's eye view point, enabling us to see the layout of the city, as it was at that time, with its gates, walls and bastions.

A later map, dated 1643 was produced by Wenceslaus Hollar (pp.10 and 11), gives a panoramic view of the city in the mid-17th century. By then, for the first time, houses were being built outside the city walls along Holywell Street, for example.

And finally, David Loggan's map of 1675 (pp.12 and 13), which enables you to see further development – an example being the construction of the Sheldonian Theatre (which is not visible on Hollar's map). The Clarendon Building, on Broad Street, was constructed in the 18th century.

For the reader and visitor alike, the plan of the city in 1250 and the maps mentioned above have been reproduced here. You will find enlargements of each map where more detail is required as you walk along beside the wall.

You will note that there are a number of bastions along the whole length of the wall. These bastions have been numbered on the 1250 plan for ease of identification.

This book is not intended to give a complete or detailed history of Oxford. Many eminent historians and archaeologists have written in depth about the city and its growth from the earliest times.

A list of further reading is given at the end of the book. This is not a definitive list, but it will help to fill some of the gaps in your knowledge of the city's history.

It is hoped that the visitor may enjoy their time whilst in Oxford, and discover parts of the city wall that are still standing and visible today.

The city

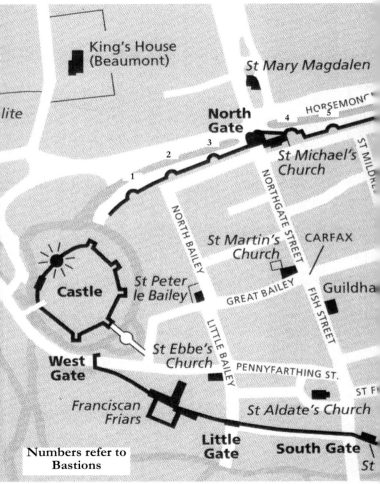

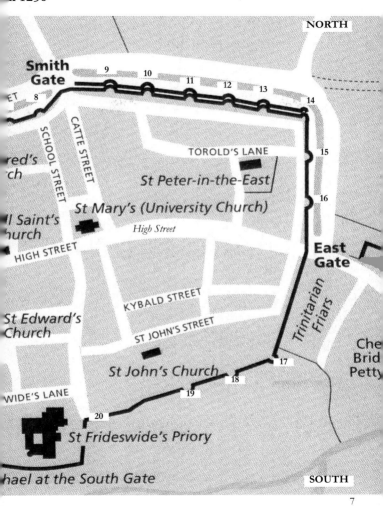

Ralph Agas's 1578 bird's

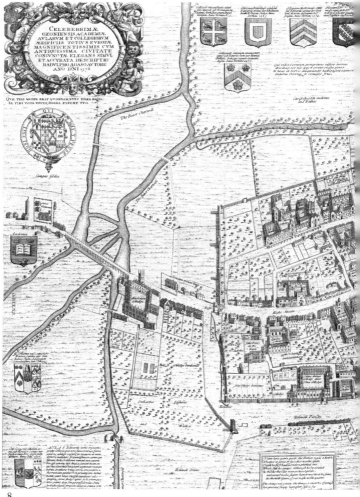

8

of Oxford from the north

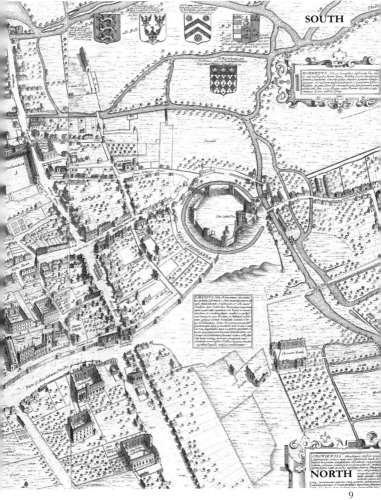

9

Wenceslaus Hollar's 164

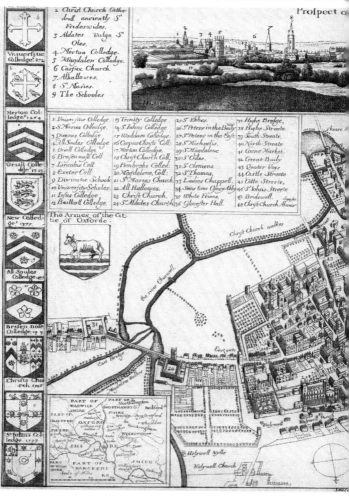

10

f Oxford from the north

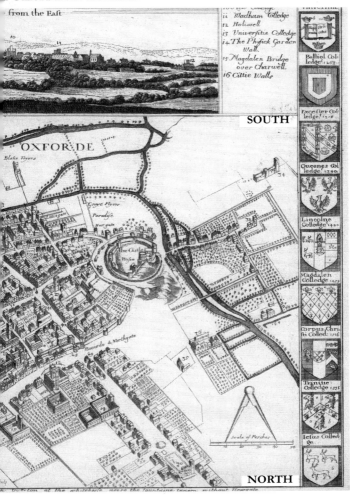

David Loggan's 1675

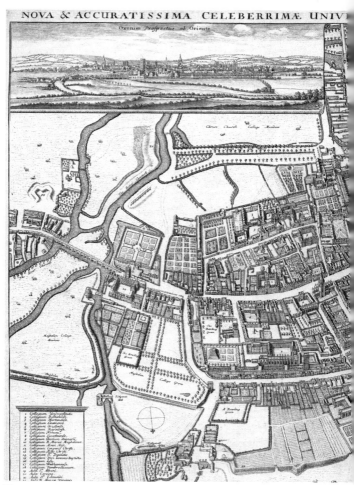

Oxford from the north

A BRIEF HISTORY OF THE WALLS

To the casual visitor Oxford may appear to be just like any other medieval city, with its glorious honey-coloured stone university buildings, churches, shops, pedestrianized streets and meadows. It is more than that. It is an ancient site, of historical, national and international importance.

But to begin at the beginning. Oxford, once a walled city, covering some 115 acres of land, lies just north of the River Thames. In the Anglo-Saxon period, Oxford was a Mercian frontier town and we know that by 911 the town already had a series of defences, mainly to the north and east, with the castle to the west and naturally defended by the Rivers Cherwell and Thames to the south.

The early defences would have been ditches with earth ramparts and palisades. It is possible that the first town defences had been built by the late 9th or early 10th century. However, by 1226 stone walls had replaced the earth ramparts, and together with bastions and gates leading into and out of the city, Oxford was well defended.

The 1250 plan of Oxford shows that there was a double defensive wall from the northern end of Catte Street to the corner of what is now Longwall Street, although a later plan does show the double defensive wall continuing to the East Gate (which spanned the High Street). This was an unusual feature in England at the time. All traces of the outer (northern) wall have long since disappeared.

Oxford was granted city status in 1524.

The city was built on a grid pattern. The main street layout has not altered significantly over the centuries, although many smaller lanes have disappeared, allowing for later development. Some street names have changed, following the change of use: for example, Cornmarket Street was known in the 15th century as North Street.

There were four town gates: North, South, East and West, each clearly identifiable on these early maps. Smaller postern gates, such as the Little Gate and Smith Gate were located at strategic points within the walls. All these gates were demolished in 1771 under the Mileways Act, allowing for easier traffic flow into the city (a problem even then).

Churches had been built near each of the main gates, only two of which are still standing – St Michael at the Northgate and St Peter in the East. The other two – St Michael at the South Gate and St Peter-le-Bailey (near the West Gate) were later demolished to make way for either college buildings, or for traffic purposes.

It would appear from all these maps that the most important entrance into the city was the North Gate, with its distinctive Saxon Tower and church dedicated to St Michael. It was here, alongside the Tower, that the famous Bocardo Prison was once located.

Much of the city wall is still visible to the visitor and it is with this in mind that the book has been compiled.

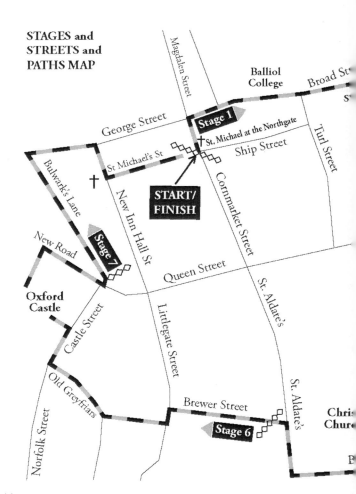

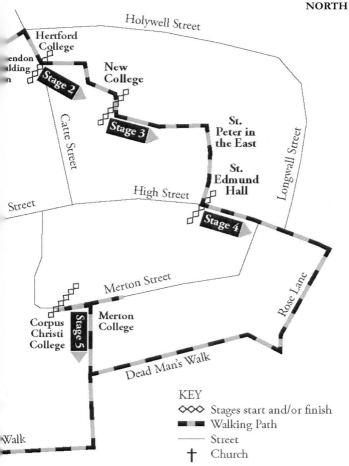

THE WALKS

There is no specific designated walk around the walls of the city. But in order to give the visitor an opportunity to see them, a number of routes have been devised to guide you.

It is possible to walk around the walls in the course of a day – perhaps allowing at least two hours in total. However, if time is limited, the full walk has been divided into seven stages, which makes it more manageable.

Some of the colleges are open to visitors, although they have different opening times. To avoid disappointment, please check the times beforehand.

Stage 1: St Michael at the Northgate to Catte Street
Starting at the church of St Michael at the Northgate, the first stage takes you along Broad Street to Catte Street, passing the Museum of Science, the Sheldonian Theatre and the Bodleian Library.

Stage 2: Catte Street to New College
This stage is a relatively short one. The wall can be seen near the Turf Tavern in St Helen's Passage. Perhaps the best preserved portion of the city wall is to be found within New College gardens.

Stage 3: New College to St Edmund Hall
From New College follow New College Lane to St Edmund Hall. St Peter in the East is now the College library and is only open to members of the College. However, the

churchyard is worth visiting. Look for St Edmund himself.

Stage 4: St Edmund Hall to Merton College

From St Edmund Hall, turn left into the High Street. Cross over and walk down on the right hand side to Rose Lane, near the Botanic Garden. This lane leads to Deadman's Walk and the city wall, which forms the southernmost boundary of Merton College.

Stage 5: Corpus Christi College to Christ Church

A portion of the city wall and a bastion can be seen in Corpus Christi College, which is to the west of Merton Grove. To reach Christ Church, walk towards Christ Church Meadow and the Broad Walk.

Stage 6: Christ Church to Oxford Castle

Although there are no signs of the wall within Christ Church, it is possible to stop off to visit the College en route to the castle. Oxford's Patron Saint, St Frideswide, is enshrined in the Lady Chapel of the Cathedral.

Stage 7: Oxford Castle to St Michael at the Northgate

The castle precinct formed the city's western boundary. Nothing now remains of the West Gate. It is possible to follow more of the wall along Bulwark's Lane into George Street, then to New Inn Hall Street and St Michael's Street which takes you back to the start of the walk.

Completion of the walk or stages is achieved by returning to Cornmarket Street, with St Michael's Church and its Tower in front of you.

Stage 1: St Michael at the Northgate to Catte Street

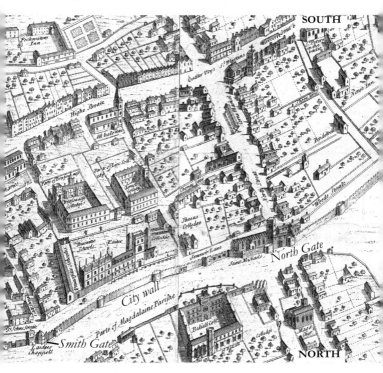

*Ralph Agas's 1578 map, showing
the North Gate, the City Wall, Smith Gate*

Stage 1: St Michael at the Northgate to Catte Street

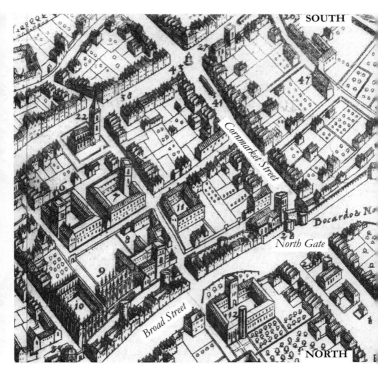

*Wenceslaus Hollar's 1643, map showing
the North Gate, the Bocardo, Cornmarket Street, Broad Street*

Stage 1: St Michael at the Northgate to Catte Street

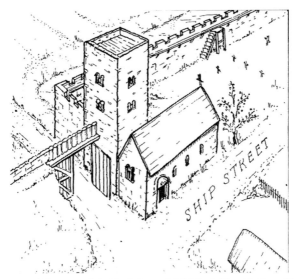

A conjectural illustration of the North Gate and St Michael's Church in Saxon Times

A church has been on this site since Domesday in 1086. The original tower was constructed as a separate building from the old Saxon church as illustrated above. The tower is still standing, and is now incorporated into the body of the church, named St Michael at the Northgate.

From the earliest maps it appears that the North Gate was the principal gated entrance into the city. The wide street of St Giles to the north, with St Giles' Church at one end and the church of St Mary Magdalen near the city gate, indicates the importance of this entry into Oxford.

Stage 1: St Michael at the Northgate to Catte Street

Tower of St Michael at the Northgate

The Tower of St Michael at the Northgate is the start of the walk. Dating back to c.1050, the Tower stood beside the ancient North Gate to the city.

To start the walk, it is worth climbing to the top of the Tower to gain a view of the city. However, no portion of the wall can be seen from this vantage point. From the base of the tower (Cornmarket Street), go to the corner and turn right into Broad Street.

Stage 1: St Michael at the Northgate to Catte Street

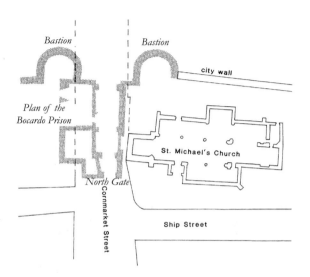

The site plan of the North Gate and the Bocardo Prison

It was at the North Gate that a prison was built in the 13th century, which became known as the Bocardo Prison. This site plan shows the extent of the prison buildings, which were mainly to the left of St Michael's Tower.

The name may have been derived from 'boccard' meaning a privy (perhaps due to its insanitary state).

The Bocardo was demolished in 1771 at the same time as the North Gate, to ease the flow of traffic into the city.

One of the bastions within the city wall formed part of the prison as can be seen on the plan.

Stage 1: St Michael at the Northgate to Catte Street

1770 illustration of St Michael's Tower, Bocardo Prison, the North Gate

Three Protestant Martyrs were interned in the Bocardo Prison and later burned at the stake (in Broad Street) between 1555 and 1556. They were Bishop Hugh Latimer and Bishop Nicholas Ridley and Archbishop Thomas Cranmer.

A small cobbled cross marking the spot is embedded in Broad Street in front of Balliol College. A plaque on the wall of Balliol College refers to their martyrdom.

Stage 1: St Michael at theNorthgate to Catte Street

Broad Street: Miss Hoskyn's garden and Bastion 5, c. 1834

Bastions were inserted into the city wall at stategic points. These semi-circular projections were set within the wall, and offered a greater degree of passive resistance for defence.

The illustration shows Bastion 5, which is located behind Boswells department store. It is, therefore, not visible from the street. Miss Hoskyns was resident in Broad Street and her garden abutted the northern side of the city wall.

Broad Street, originally known as Canditch, a deep moat, and then later as Horsemonger Lane.

Stage 1: St Michael at theNorthgate to Catte Street

Broad Street and the City Wall

Entering Broad Street, continue along the right hand side. A narrow opening near The Tourist Information Centre leads into a small yard, where a portion of the city wall is visible. Although Bastion 5 cannot be seen from here, it is still in existence and is now an annexe of Jesus College (founded in 1571 by Dr Hugh Price).

Retrace your steps into Broad Street, turn right and continue east along the street.

Stage 1: St Michael at the Northgate to Catte Street

Broad Street, showing the Sheldonian Theatre and the Clarendon Building

Broad Street, which is now partly pedestrianized, lies over the Canditch (or city ditch) which was infilled and paved by 1675.

The buildings on the northern side of Broad Street comprise Balliol College (founded in 1263 by John de Balliol); Trinity College (founded in 1555 by Sir Thomas Pope); Blackwell's Bookshop, founded in 1879 by Benjamin Blackwell and the New Bodleian Library, designed by Gilbert Scott, and completed in 1940.

The southern side of the Street includes shops, Exeter College and a number of university buildings.

Stage 1: St Michael at the Northgate to Catte Street

Broad Street, showing Balliol College

Continue along Broad Street. You will be walking parallel to the city wall which is located behind the shops and offices.

Balliol and Trinity Colleges are on the left hand side of the road, and are open to the public. Check opening times with the Lodge Porters in both instances.

The colleges are well worth visiting and give a further insight into the lives of students studying in Oxford.

Stage 1: St Michael at the Northgate to Catte Street

Broad Street, Bastion 6, c. 1834

Bastion 6 is now incorporated within The Tower House Hotel, a small hotel located in Ship Street, which runs parallel to Broad Sreet. The outside of this bastion can be seen by walking down a small alleyway in Broad Street – see the opposite page. You will notice that it has changed little over time.

The city wall continued to Turl Street, where there was a 'twirling' gate (demolished in 1722). No trace of this gate now remains (p.32).

Many of the city fortifications had fallen into disuse by the 1600s.

Stage 1: St Michael at the Northgate to Catte Street

Broad Street, Bastion 6

Still in Broad Street, Bastion 6 can be found in the garden at the rear of a small sandwich shop. Part of the city wall can also be seen here, before it 'disappears' eastwards towards Turl Street.

At this point, the wall was demolished to make way for Exeter College, founded in 1314 by Walter de Stapledon (p.32); the Museum of the History of Science (once the Old Ashmolean Museum) and the Sheldonian Theatre.

Stage 1: St Michael at the Northgate to Catte Street

Line of the demolished city wall showing the site of the Turl Gate

- - - - - = **demolished city wall**

Stage 1: St Michael at the Northgate and Catte Street

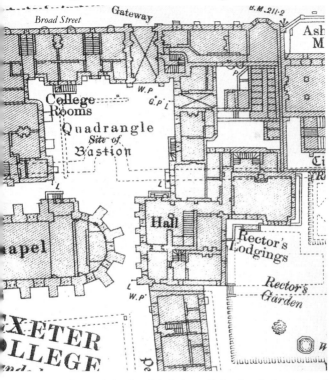

Line of the demolished city wall showing the bastion in the quadrangle of Exeter College and main gateway in 1878

Stage 1: St Michael at the Northgate and Catte Street

The Museum of the History of Science, c. 1834

Built between 1679-83 this is perhaps one of the finest 17th century buildings in Oxford.

The building originally housed Elias Ashmole's collection of artefacts, inherited from John Tradescant the Younger. The Museum became the School of Natural History and was the first chemical laboratory in England.

Ashmole's collections soon outgrew the space within the building and were moved to the new Ashmolean Museum in Beaumont Street, in 1845.

The History of Science Museum is open to visitors.

Stage 1: St Michael at the Northgate Street to Catte Street

Exeter College main gateway into Broad Street, c.1834

This gateway was inserted in the city wall, and was at one time the main entrance into Exeter College as marked on the plan on p.33.

It is possible to visit the College – check with the Porter's Lodge in Turl Street – now the main entrance to the College.

Continue walking towards the Sheldonian Theatre, passing the Museum of Science on your right. Look for the ceremonial entrance to the Museum, as shown on the left of the print on the opposite page.

Stage 1: St Michael at the Northgate to Catte Street

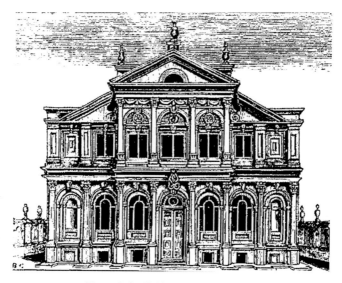

Front of the Sheldonian Theatre, c. 1834

The Sheldonian Theatre, designed by Sir Christopher Wren and built between 1664-7, is still used throughout the year for the awarding of academic degrees. The Encaenia is a major university ceremony and takes place in the theatre in June at the end of Trinity Term.

The Emperors' Heads, which surmount the theatre railings, dated to 1669, although they were replaced in 1970.

Oxford has been the home of printing since 1478. The printing presses belonging to the university were once housed in the Theatre.

Stage 1: St Michael at the Northgate to Cattd Street

The Sheldonian Theatre

The Sheldonian Theatre is open to the public on certain days throughout the year. It is well worth visiting. Climb up to the cupola for some fine city views.

The Bodleian Library, which opened in 1602, now occupies many of the surrounding buildings. It is one of five Copyright Libraries in Britain. Over 5 million books are stored on shelving in the surrounding buildings. Visitors are welcome.

Stage 1: St Michael at the Northgate to Catte Street

The Clarendon Building, c. 1834, facing Broad Street

Designed by Nicholas Hawksmoor in 1712-13, the Clarendon Press, as it was then known, was built with the proceeds from the Earl of Clarendon's *History of the Great Rebellion* (1702-4).

Originally built to house the University Press, this magnificent building now forms part of the Bodleian Library complex. The University Press outgrew these premises and moved to Walton Street in 1832.

The Muses on the roof of the building are by James Thornhill and mainly date to 1717.

Stage 1: St Michael at the Northgate to Catte Street

The Clarendon Building, facing the Bodleian Quadrangle

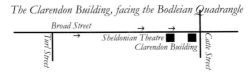

The Clarendon Building was built on the site of houses adjacent to the Sheldonian Theatre, which were demolished to make way for it.

David Loggan's map of 1675 (pp.12 and 13) shows this area very clearly. Although the city wall had been demolished by this time, it had turned north behind the building to meet the gate at the northern end of Catte Street. This gate was known as Smith Gate (p.43).

Catte Street was originally known as St Catharine Street.

Stage 1: St Michael at the Northgate to Catte Street

Chapel of Our Lady St Catharine, 1521

The city wall then continued eastwards from the corner of Catte Street to Longwall Street. Two parallel walls were built, the outer one known as the Town Wall (which has since disappeared), and the inner one, known as New College Wall, which is still in existence (pp.6 and 7).

It appears that this double defensive set of walls was very unsual in England at the time – c. 1250.

The small chapel of St Catharine may have been built on the site of a bastion in 1521. Hollar refers to it as the 'Ladies Chapell'. Although much altered, the chapel is now part of Hertford College. The stone panel dates from 1521.

Stage 1: St Michael at the Northgate to Catte Street

Octagonal Building, Hertford College

Walking from the Clarendon Building into Catte Street, you will see an octagonal 'chapel'. The 1521 panel is over the door.

The building immediately to the left of the 'chapel' is the old Indian Institute – note the elephants on the tower.

From this point in Catte Street, cross the road into New College Lane. Proceed under the 'Bridge of Sighs' and then turn left into a narrow passageway, now known as St Helen's Passage.

Stage 2: Catte Street to New College

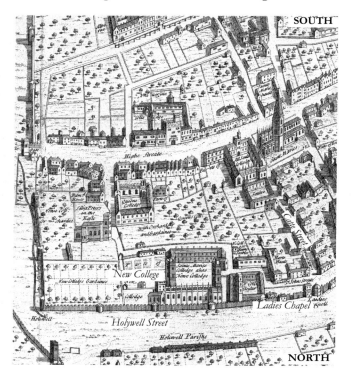

*Ralph Agas's map of 1578, showing,
Catte Street, Ladies Chapel, Holywell Street*

Stage 2: Catte Street to New College

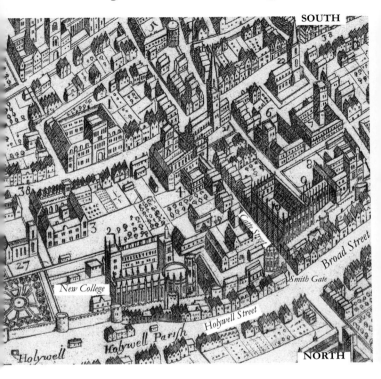

Wenceslaus Hollar's map of 1643, showing Broad Street, Catte Street, Smith Gate, Holywell Street

Stage 2: Catte Street to New College

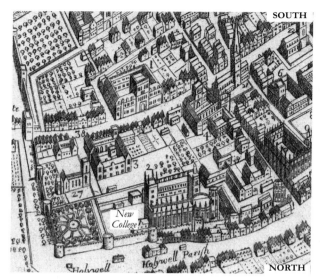

Wenceslaus Hollar's map of 1643, showing New College (1379)

Hollar's map shows the area between Catte Street (Smith Gate) and Holywell Street in greater detail.

Of the two defensive walls, the northernmost one, known as the Town Wall had been demolished by 1643. The wall that you can see here is New College Wall (p.43).

Note the building development along both the city wall, and Holywell Street – all of which had taken place between 1578 and 1643

Holywell Street, originally known as Canditch (the town rubbish ditch), had been infilled allowing for such building.

Stage 2: Catte Street to New College

The City Wall at St Helen's Passage

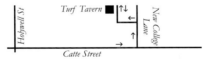

St Helen's Passage leads to the Turf Tavern. The city wall is on your right as you walk down to the tavern. You pass a much altered Bastion 9, with a spiral staircase, also on your right.

This famous pub abuts the outer city wall, which now continues straight towards New College. The Bell Tower that you can see from the tavern is adjacent to the College cloisters.

Stop for a while before retracing your steps to New College Lane.

Stage 2: Catte Street to New College

New College entrance, c. 1834

New College was founded in 1379 by William of Wykeham. 'He bought the land here in 1369 . . . an area reduced by plague to being, full of filth, dirt and stinking carcasses . . . a place as 'twere desolate . . .'.

The full name of the College is St Mary of Winchester at Oxford'. It is now known as 'New College' to distinguish it from Oriel College (1326), which is also dedicated to the Virgin Mary.

A major part of the existing city wall can be found in the College grounds.

Stage 2: Catte Street to New College

New College entrance gateway

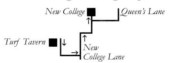

Turn left into New College Lane, noting the 1402 tithe barn on your right (p.59). The entrance to the College is directly ahead. There is usually a small entry charge.

The Front Quad is the first place you enter. Turn left into the cloisters. You will pass the College chapel on your right.

Stroll around the cloisters, noting the plaques to famous old students as you go. The tree in the cloister is a Quercus Ilex.

Stage 2: Catte Street to New College

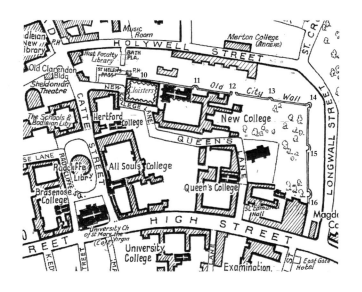

*Map of Oxford, showing
Catte Street, St Helen's Passage, New College*

Stage 2: Catte Street to New College

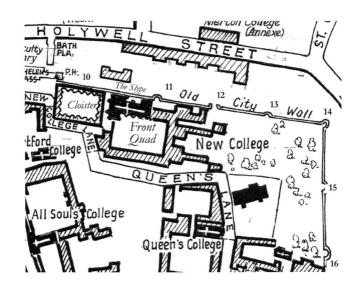

Enlarged map of New College Garden, showing the Bastions, the City Wall, Holywell Street

Stage 2: Catte Street to New College

New College Cloisters, c. 1834

The cloisters were built some ten years after the main College buildings, and were not part of the original college design. The roof of the cloisters is original.

The north cloister is built on a part of a common lane which ran along the inside of the New College wall. The crenellated bell tower was built in 1396 and stands on the site of Bastion 10.

The map on p. 48 shows that the bastions were built about sixty yards apart and are well defined. Semi-circular bastions were used throughout the 16th century.

Stage 2: Catte Street to New College

The North Wall of New College Cloisters

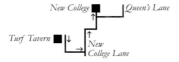

New College chapel is one of the largest in Oxford, and should not be missed. Do not forget to notice the imposing reredos on the east wall. Lift up one or two of the seats in the 14th century oak choir stalls to see the misericords with their quaint carvings underneath.

The glass in the antechapel is worth noting. The west window dates to 1778, and is by Joshua Reynolds. The sculpture of Lazarus is by Jacob Epstein (1951).

Stage 2: Catte Street to New College

New College Garden with Ramparts

The College gardens are delightful. The herbaceous borders show the wall at its best. The original ramparts, and open bastions set within the walls, are an unusual feature.

The upkeep and maintenance of the walls are the responsibility of the College. Tradition has it that the walls are inspected every three years by the Mayor of Oxford – a ritual going back to 1379.

The mound in the centre of the garden was created about 1594 and is unique. Summer dramatics are performed annually within the garden.

Stage 2: Catte Street to New College

New College Garden, with Bastion 13

Re-enter the Front Quad from the chapel. Cross this quad into the Garden Quad. At the far end of this Quad, the gardens open out in front of you.

Go through the wrought iron gate following the path to your left. Continue along this garden path, passing Bastion 14, which marks the corner of the wall as it turns south. Bastion 16 marks the boundary between New College and St Edmund Hall (p.60).

Stage 2: Catte Street to New College

The Slype, New College, c. 1834

This illustration clearly shows the Bell Tower, although at a precarious angle, with a portion of the New College wall. The pinnacled building on the left is the College chapel.

Note the encroachment of buildings, built somewhat randomly, close up to the wall. This area, known as The Slype, was the space between the two defensive city walls. It is still known by that name today.

New College expanded its intake of students in the 1800s, resulting in these old tenement houses being demolished, togther with a number in Holywell Street.

Stage 2: Catte Street to New College

Gateway in New College and Gateway (Bastion 12)

It is not always possible to view the outer side of the wall within the College. It is worth asking the Lodge Porter at the Holywell Street entrance to the College for permission to do so.

The above gateway can then be easily seen from the Porter's Lodge. This gate was originally one of the bastions and now forms a link between both parts of the College.

The area known as The Slype is to the left of this illustrated map.

Stage 3: New College to St Edmund Hall

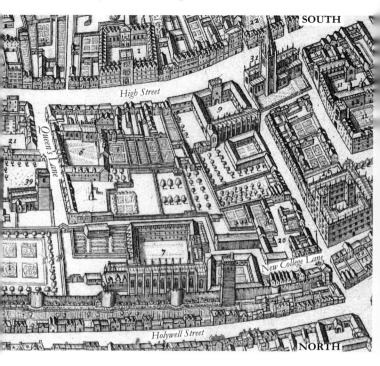

*David Loggan's map of 1675, showing
New College Lane, Holywell Street, Queen's Lane*

Stage 3: New College to St Edmund Hall

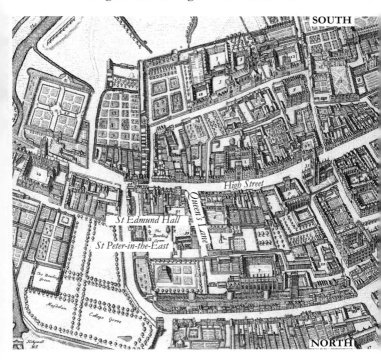

*David Loggan's map of 1675, showing
Queen's Lane, St Peter-in-the-East, St Edmund Hall*

Stage 3: New College to St Edmund Hall

New College Lane/Queen's Lane

Some Oxford street names have been altered over the centuries. The streets may, for example, have just been known by the name of a person living there at the time. One such is Torold's Lane (as mentioned in the 1250 map), but now known as Queen's Lane.

The lane is an extension of New College Lane, and begins under the archway featured above. It runs at the back of Queen's College (founded by Robert Eglesfeld in 1340) and New College.

It provides access from Broad Street, via Catte Street, to the High Street and is not open to through traffic.

Stage 3: New College to St Edmund Hall

New College Lane and the 1402 Tithe Barn

Retrace your steps to the entrance in New College Lane, turn left under the archway and follow the lane behind The Queen's College.

As you go down Queen's Lane look upwards to your left to see the grotesques on the buildings of New College. The masons were given a 'free' hand when they carved these faces.

The church on the left is St Peter-in-the-East, and is now part of St Edmund Hall, which is the next stop along the walk.

Stage 3: New College to St Edmund Hall

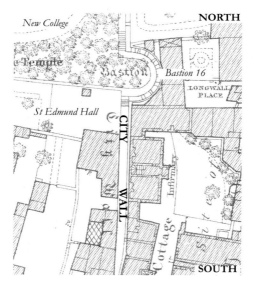

St Edmund Hall, c.1881

The Hall is named after St Edmund of Abingdon, Archbishop of Canterbury from 1234-40, who resided and taught in this area of Oxford.

The origins of the Hall go back to the 13th century. However, from the 16th century, the Hall was administered by Queen's College, but early in the 20th century there was a gradual transfer of powers to the Hall itself.

The city wall extends into the college grounds south from New College, as the above illustration shows. The wall then continued to the East Gate in the High Street.

Stage 3: New College to St Edmund Hall

St Edmund Hall Lower Quad

The entrance to the Hall is on the left, just beyond the church.

The Hall is open to the public. To view the wall, go through the Front Quad and into the Lower Quad. The city wall can be seen at the far end of this quadrangle. It can be identified by the ramparts of Bastion 16 and marks the boundary with New College.

This is the last sighting of the city wall until we reach Merton College.

Stage 3: New College to St Edmund Hall

St Peter-in-the-East

St Peter-in-the-East is one of only two churches still standing that were built near the city gates. First recorded in 1086, the church replaced an earlier timber-framed building.

The church was built by Grymbald in the reign of King Alfred the Great – the crypt being the oldest part.

The church is now the library of St Edmund Hall, the interior of which was altered to meet the demands of a modern library. The exterior remains more or less unaltered. The tower has been converted into a book store.

Pevsner is reported to have said that this church is 'without doubt the most interesting church of Oxford'.

Stage 3: New College to St Edmund Hall

St Peter-in-the-East - Churchyard

This lovely church stands within its own grounds and forms an intrinsic part of the Hall. The library is not open to the public, but it is possible to walk around the churchyard. Some interesting tombs to note: James Sadler, the first English air balloonist (1753-1828), and Sarah Hounslow whose death is recorded as 31st February 1835.

There is a modern sculpture of St Edmund of Abingdon sitting on a tomb.

Stage 4: St Edmund Hall to Merton College

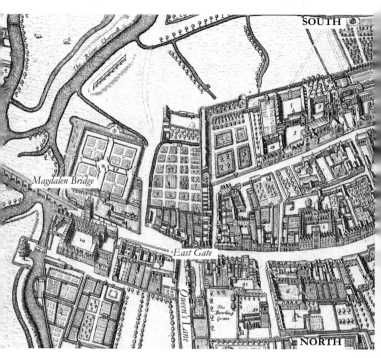

David Loggan's map of 1675, showing
Queen's Lane, the East Gate, Magdalen Bridge

Stage 4: St Edmund Hall to Merton College

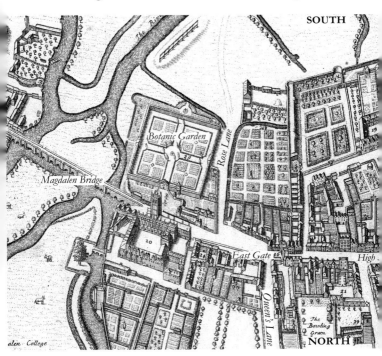

David Loggan's map of 1675, showing
The High Street, the East Gate, Rose Lane, the Botanic Garden

Stage 4: St Edmund Hall to Merton College

The East Gate, c. 1668

The wall continued southwards from St Edmund Hall, until it reached the East Gate, which then spanned the High Street, as shown in the above illustration.

The site of the gate was near where the Eastgate Hotel is now situated.

The main route from the east entered the city here – the road crossing the River Cherwell at various points over Magdalen Bridge.

The East Gate was demolished in 1771-2, along with the other city gates, to make way for improvements to the traffic flow in and out of the city.

Stage 4: St Edmund Hall to Merton College

The East Gate plaque

Turning left out of St Edmund Hall, walk towards the High Street – a matter of yards – and turn left at the corner of Queen's Lane. Cross the road here and walk to the Eastgate Hotel. Note the plaque on the hotel wall in the High Street, which gives an idea of what the East Gate looked like.

Continue down the High Street until you reach Rose Lane on your right. Turn right here. The Botanic Garden will be on your left.

Stage 4: St Edmund Hall to Merton College

Merton College Gate

Merton College is Oxford's oldest college (although some may dispute it). Walter de Merton, twice Chancellor of England, bought the land within the southern part of the city wall and founded his college in 1264. The statutes of this foundation made provision for 30-40 graduate Fellows.

The College chapel was the parish church of St John the Baptist, serving the local population. Note the various plaques on the walls in the antechapel.

Merton College has the distinction of being the primary model for most of the colleges within Oxford and Cambridge.

Stage 4: St Edmund Hall to Merton College

Deadman's Walk from Merton College Garden

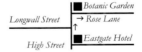

At the far end of Rose Lane, go through the large gates, keeping to your right along a gravel path. This is known as Deadman's Walk.

Note the plaque to James Sadler, who made his first balloon ascent from the meadow here on 4th October 1784.

The wall that is now on your right is part of the city wall and Merton College. The College garden is on the other side of the wall.

Continue to the end of the path turning right through an iron gate.

Stage 4: St Edmund Hall to Merton College

Deadman's Walk, early print

Oxford's Jewish quarter lay mainly in the area between Carfax and the South Gate. By 1190 two Jewish cemeteries were located near Magdalen Bridge. Magdalen College now occupies one site and the Botanic Garden the other site.

A path, known as Deadman's Walk, which skirted the southern part of the city wall, had been constructed in about 1081. It was used by the Jewish community to take their dead for burial in either of these two cemeteries (or maybe to Cripplegate in London), as they were forbidden to carry the corpses through the Christian city of Oxford.

Stage 4: St Edmund Hall to Merton College

Deadman's Walk and Bastion 19 at Merton College

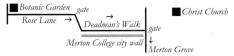

You will notice the reduced height of the walls compared to those in New College. Merton Fields and Christ Church Meadow are on your left as you walk towards the iron gate and into Merton Grove (p.72).

At the end of Merton Grove, turn right into Merton Street. Merton College entrance is on your right. The College is open only in the afternoons. The smallest quadrangle in Oxford is here in Merton. It is possible to see the city wall by entering the Fellows' Quad.

Stage 5: Merton College to Christ Church

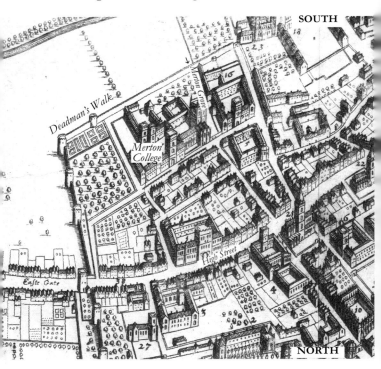

*Wenceslaus Hollar's map of 1643, showing
Deadman's Walk, Merton College, Merton Grove*

Stage 5: Merton College to Christ Church

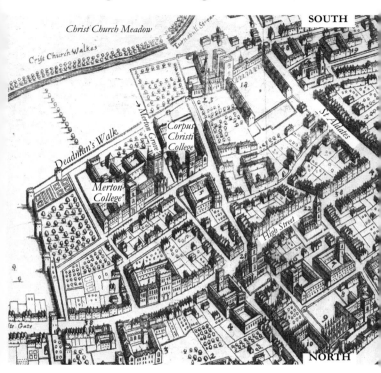

*Wenceslaus Hollar's map of 1643, showing
Merton Grove, Corpus Christi College, Christ Church Meadow*

Stage 5: Merton College to Chirst Church

Corpus Christi College

Corpus Christi College was founded in 1513 by Richard Fox, Bishop of Winchester. This small and intimate college is located between Merton Street and the city wall.

Note the pillar sundial which stands in the centre of the Front Quad. Known as the Pelican Sundial, it was erected in 1581 by Charles Turnbull.

The direction of the city wall now runs westwards and forms the boundary between Corpus Christi College and Christ Church.

A large bastion is visible in the gardens and is the last remaining one along this section of the wall.

Stage 5: Merton College to Christ Church

Corpus Christi College and Bastion 20

From Merton College turn left and enter Corpus Christi College via the Porter's Lodge. The College is open only in the afternoons.

The city wall forms the College's southern boundary with Christ Church and can be viewed from the College gardens. Bastion 20 is now incorporated into the College's conference centre.

Leaving Corpus Christi, turn right and retrace your steps through Merton Grove towards Christ Church Meadow.

Stage 5: Merton College to Christ Church

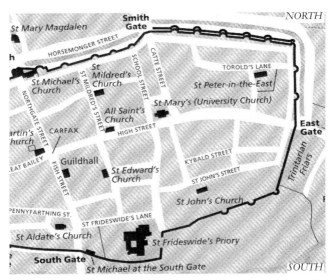

Map of Oxford dated c. 1250, showing St Frideswide's Priory

Christ Church College now incorporates the site of St Frideswide's Priory, which dates back to the 12th century.

It was an important priory, although it lost its significance after the Dissolution of the monasteries between 1536-41.

Cardinal Wolsey, Henry VIII's Chancellor, began to build Cardinal College before he fell from grace in 1529. He never completed the task. Henry VIII refounded the College in 1532, renaming it Christ Church.

The church of St Michael at the South Gate, marked on the above map, was razed to the ground to make way for the College buildings.

Stage 5: Merton College to Christ Church

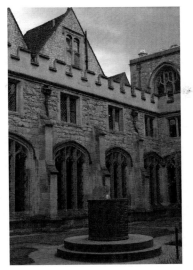

Chrish Church Cloister, once part of St Frideswide's Priory (c. 703)

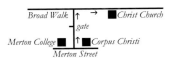

Walk south towards the River Thames and Christ Church Meadow. You will pass a wrought iron gate on your right, through which it is possible to see Oxford's Cathedral.

St Frideswide, the patron saint of Oxford, is enshrined within the Cathedral.

It is possible to visit Christ Church and the Cathedral – the entrance is via the Meadow Building on your right.

Stage 5: Merton College to Christ Church

Christ Church Hall and Memorial Garden

Henry's new foundation also incorporated the Dean and Chapter of the new diocese of Oxford. This unusual combination means that the cathedral is also the College chapel.

Oxford was granted city status in 1524, thus enabling a new diocese to be created out of the Diocese of Lincoln.

Robert King (Suffragan Bishop of Lincoln and the last Abbot of Osney) became Bishop in 1542. The abbey was then abandoned after this turn of events.

The Bishop's Palace can be seen directly opposite the entrance to the Memorial Garden.

Stage 5: Merton College to Christ Church

Tom Tower at Christ Church, St Aldate's

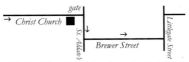

Leaving Christ Church, walk through the Memorial Gardens west towards the main street named St Aldate's.

The South Gate was located at the very corner of the College buildings. It was removed in the late 17th century, along with the church of St Michael at the South Gate.

As you leave the Memorial Garden turn right, cross the road, and after a few yards, turn left into Brewer Street.

79

Stage 6: Christ Church to Oxford Castle

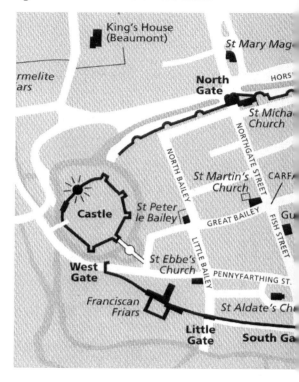

1250 map of Oxford, showing the site of the Little Gate

Stage 6: Christ Church to Oxford Castle

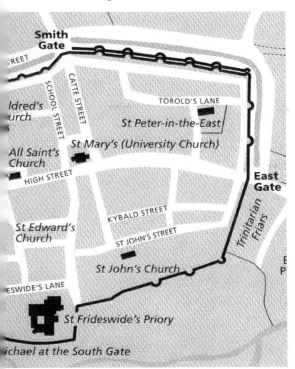

1250 map of Oxford, showing the site of St Frideswide's Priory

Stage 6: Christ Church to Oxford Castle

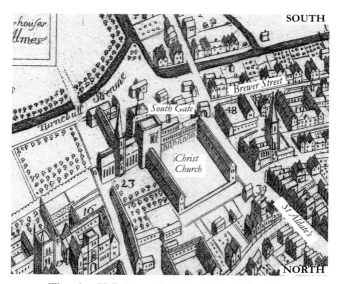

Wenceslaus Hollar's map of 1643, showing the South Gate

The above map of Oxford shows the South Gate in situ in 1643. By 1675 it had been removed to make way for the building of Wolsey's college, then known as Cardinal College.

The church of St Michael at the South Gate was situated near the South Gate. As the parish was small, it was deemed convenient to demolish it to make way for the college buildings.

Christ Church Cathedral School, established in 1546, for the free education of fourteen boy choristers, is located in Brewer Street. The School still educates children today.

Stage 6: Christ Church to Oxford Castle

The City Wall along Brewer Street looking west

Brewer Street takes its name from the number of breweries which were operating here in 1620. The city wall is on your right.

Walk to the end of this street, noting Campion Hall (Edwin Lutyens's only building in Oxford) on your left.

Note the new footbridge at the end of the street, linking parts of Pembroke College. The College (founded by King James I in 1624) is behind the wall on your right. The College is not open to the public.

Stage 6: Christ Church to Oxford Castle

The Church of St Peter-le-Bailey, near the West Gate, c. 1863

The site of this church is Bonn Square, at the northern end of St Ebbe's Street. It was one of the 'gate' churches. - and was near to the West Gate of the city.

The church tower collapsed in 1726, resulting in the church being rebuilt in 1740. But in 1874, to ease the traffic flow into what is now Queen Street, the church was again demolished. Nothing now remains of the church of St Peter-le-Bailey on its original site.

However, to confuse matters, in 1874 a new church, using the same name, was built in New Inn Hall Street. This is now the chapel of St Peter's College.

Stage 6: Christ Church to Oxford Castle

THIS IS THE SITE OF THE FORMER
LITTLEGATE. SOMETIMES KNOWN AS
LITTLE SOUTH GATE FIRST MENTIONED
IN 1244 AND ONE OF THE SEVEN
MEDIEVAL GATES OF THE CITY OF
OXFORD.   EXCAVATIONS IN 1971
AND 1972 UNCOVERED THE FOOTINGS
OF THE WEST SIDE OF THE GATE
AND THE 13TH CENTURY CITY WALL

The story of the Little Gate

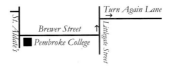

Walk to the end of Brewer Street and you will come to Littlegate Street. Originally known as Little Bailey, this street runs north to Bonn Square and south towards the River Thames.

As you emerge from Brewer Street, note the above plaque which is on the wall of the building opposite you.

There is nothing left of the city wall or the Little Gate at this point. Turn left and then immediately right into Turn Again Lane.

Stage 6: Christ Church to Oxford Castle

Illustration of the Little Gate, c. 1791

The Little Gate was one of the smaller gates into the city. It was situated at the southern end of St Ebbe's and Littlegate Street. The location of the Little Gate is noted on the map dated 1250 (pp.80-81). The city wall can be traced reasonably easily as it runs in a more or less straight line from the South Gate.

A small portion of the wall is still visible, although hard to find as it constitutes a back wall in a garden in Turn Again Lane.

There were two friaries in this part of Oxford which were demolished during the Dissolution of the monasteries.

Stage 6: Christ Church to Oxford Castle

Littlegate Street looking south

Continue down Turn Again Lane, and then turn up a small passageway named Roger Bacon Lane. Part of the existing wall can be seen, from above, by peering over the wall and looking down into the back garden of the first house (No. 10).

Retrace your steps and turn right. Note the old 17th century houses on your right – and the plaque on the wall. These houses were rescued from demoliton in the 1960s.

Stage 6: Christ Church to Oxford Castle

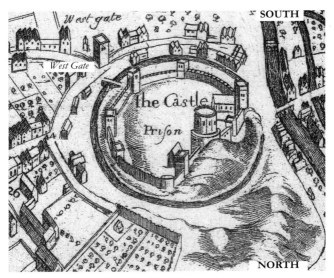

Wenceslaus Hollar's map of 1643, showing the West Gate and Castle

The castle formed the western boundary of the city wall and defences. The location of the West Gate is shown above, adjoining the castle moat.

The castle, built by Robert d'Oilly in 1071 for William the Conqueror, covered approximately 2.5 acres. It is a prime site rising above the marshes and the Rivers Thames and Cherwell.

The castle moat was supplied with water from the River Thames. Two bridges crossed the moat leading into the castle, one going towards the town and the other towards the west from St George's Tower.

Stage 6: Christ Church to Oxford Castle

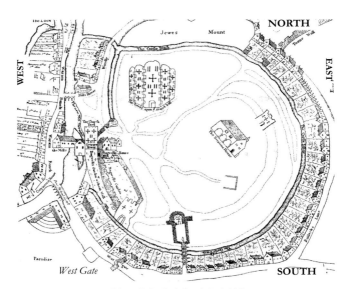

Plan of Oxford Castle in 1616

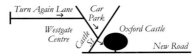

From Turn Again Lane proceed west, past the car park and turn right into Castle Street. Cross the road after The Castle Tavern and Paradise Street – the entrance to the castle complex is on your left.

As you enter the precincts, turn left, and walk down some steps to view part of the Saxon wall. Note the plaque which depicts the outline of Oxford's Saxon defences.

Continue in a clockwise direction to see the old gaol (now a hotel).

Stage 6: Christ Church to Oxford Castle

The Castle Mound, c. 1668

The castle has played a strategic role in the defence of Oxford throughout the centuries. During the English Civil War (1642-46), it became a military base.

From the earliest times, however, a gaol or prison had been built within the precincts. Robert d'Oilly also founded the collegiate church of St George in 1074 on this site. Only the crypt now remains.

It is believed that St George's Tower dates back to Saxon times.

A well can be found beneath the castle mound and has withstood the ravages of time.

Stage 6: Christ Church to Oxford Castle

St George's Tower, Castle Complex

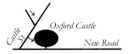

Leaving the Saxon wall area, continue walking round the back of the old prison, which is now the Malmaison Hotel.

The old cell blocks that you see here are now mainly hotel rooms.

A visitor centre, known as 'Oxford Castle Unlocked' offers an insight into the history of the castle site and the prison. Climb to the top of St George's Tower for a city view.

Take time to walk up the mound and look for the well.

Stage 6: Christ Church to Oxford Castle

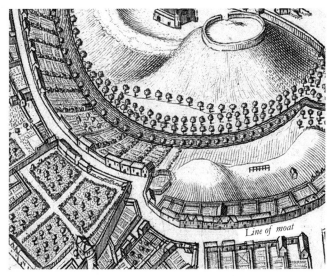

David Loggan's map of 1675, showing the silted moat

Over the centuries the moat silted up. Between 1643 and 1675 most of the castle had fallen into disrepair

The gaol was still in use as a prison, and continued to function as such until 1996.

From 1578 and until at least 1643, the castle moat was part of the defences of the city. However, by 1675 both the inner and outer banks of the moat had been built upon. This is clearly shown in the above illustration.

Two interesting facts: the last outside hanging took place in 1863, and the last internal hanging took place in 1952.

Stage 6: Christ Church to Oxford Castle

Prison 'cells' now part of an hotel

Following the closure of the prison in 1996, the castle area was sold. The prison itself was later turned into a hotel in 2006. Major excavations on the castle site took place during the intervening period.

Leave the castle complex via New Road. Turn right, crossing the street and turn left into Bulwark's Lane. This small lane runs along the back of St Peter's College, which is on your right.

The city wall curved north at this point.

Stage 7: Oxford Castle to St Michael in the Northgate

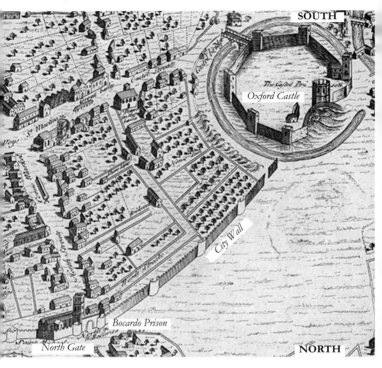

*Ralph Agas's map of 1578, showing
Oxford Castle, City Wall, the Bocardo Prison, the North Gate*

Stage 7: Oxford Castle to St Michael in the Northgate

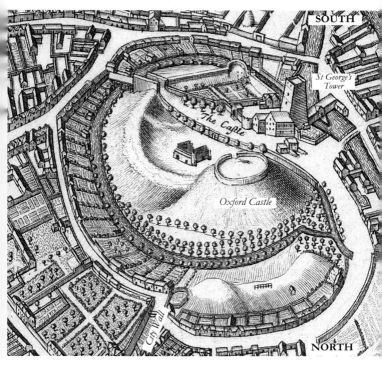

*David Loggan's map of 1675, showing
Oxford Castle, St George's Tower, City Wall*

Stage 7: Oxford Castle to St Michael at the Northgate

Bulwark's Lane

From Ralph Agas's map of 1578 it is possible to see where the city wall continued its route towards the North Gate. It is also evident from these early maps, that there were many gardens or orchards within the city walls.

Oxford has been a seat of learning since at least the 10th century, with the University being established before the 13th century.

Many small halls and monastic houses were operating during these early times and some of these were later incorporated into the colleges of today.

Stage 7: Oxford Castle to St Michael at the Northgate

History Faculty Building, George Street

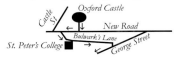

Walk to the end of Bulwark's Lane. Turn right here into George Street. Continue walking on the right hand side of the road.

You come to the History Faculty, which was built as the City of Oxford High School in 1880. One famous pupil of the school was T.E. Lawrence, later known as Lawrence of Arabia.

On the left side of the road is the Old Fire Station, the bus station and Gloucester Green market place.

Stage 7: Oxford Castle to St Michael at the Northgate

Bastion 3 of the city wall, looking west

The city wall curved northwards from Bulwark's Lane, having three bastions along its length, before reaching the North Gate.

The last major part of the wall, and the base of Bastion 3 can still be seen in the garden of the History Faculty.

New Inn Hall Street (originally known as North Bailey (by 1399), and from c.1550 to 1800 as the Lane of the Seven Deadly Sins, was extended into George Street in 1872. This street runs parallel to Cornmarket Street.

The New Inn Hall was eventually incorporated into St Peter's College.

Stage 7: Oxford Castle to St Michael at the Northgate

Bastion 3, looking east

Turn right from George Street into New Inn Hall Street. Access to the History Faculty garden is via a small narrow path on your right just before the Methodist church. It is possible to walk along the path to the end of the wall. Note the blocked window in the side of the lower part of this bastion.

Retrace your steps to New Inn Hall Street. Cross the road and walk down St Michael's Street.

Stage 7: Oxford Castle to St Michael at the Northgate

St Michael's Street looking east

The northern section of the city wall from the castle to St Michael in the Northgate is not long.

St Michael's Street is one of the original Saxon streets, linking New Inn Hall Street to Cornmarket Street.

At the far end of St Michael's Street, the sites of the Bocardo Prison and the North Gate lie beneath the buildings on the left side of the street. All we have are the ground plans which show of their existence (p.24).

The Tower of St Michael's church was joined at some point to the Bocardo Prison. It is all that now remains from the Saxon period in this area of Oxford.

Stage 7: Oxford Castle to St Michael at the Northgate

St Michael's Street looking west

Continue walking to the end of St Michael's Street. As you walk along, it is possible to see a remnant or two of the city wall, for example, at the rear of the Vanbrugh Hotel.

At the end of this street you will come to a crossroads, with St Michael's Tower (where your journey began), directly in front of you.

You have now completed the circuit around the city walls of Oxford.

FURTHER READING

To source further information on the walls, the colleges, the castle and other notable buildings a list is given below of books, pamphlets and other archival material.

Green, V.H.H., *The Tower and Church of St Michael at the North Gate* (Guide Book)

Hassall, T.G., Oxford, *The Buried City* (Oxford Archaeological Unit, Oxford, 1998)

Hibbert, C., and Hibbert, E., (eds.), *The Encyclopaedia of Oxford* (Macmillan, 1988)

Ingram, J., *Memorials of Oxford*, Vols I, II, III (Parker, 1834)

Oxoniensia IV, 1939, p. 159

Oxoniensia VIII-IX, 1943-44, p. 159

Oxoniensia XVI, 1959, p. 29

Oxoniensia, XXXVI, 1971, p. 9

Oxoniensia XLI 1976, pp. 148-161

Salter, H.E., *The Historical Names of the Streets & Lanes of Oxford*, Intra Muros (Oxford, 1921)

Sherwood, J., and Pevsner, N., *The Buildings of England, Oxfordshire* (Harmondsworth, 1974)

Tyack, G., *Oxford. An Architectural Guide* (Oxford, 1998)

Victoria County History, *A History of the County of Oxford*, Vol. 4, The City of Oxford

PHOTOGRAPHS AND ILLUSTRATIONS

All the photographs were taken by Priscilla Frost.

Illustrations and maps have been reproduced from various sources:

The plans of the Saxon Tower at St Michael at the Northgate and Bocardo Prison were reproduced with the permission of the Oxford Archaeological Unit

The 1250 plan of Oxford has been reproduced with the permission of the Oxford University Press

The map of Oxford, c. 1961, was produced with the permission of G.I. Barnett and Son Ltd

The maps of Ralph Agas, Wenceslaus Hollar and David Loggan were reproduced with the permission of John Leighfield

Other illustrations were reproduced with the permission of The Centre of Oxfordshire Studies, Oxford

ACKNOWLEDGMENTS

I am indebted to Helen Drury of the Centre for Oxfordshire Studies, who helped me locate many of the illustrations and her unfailing patience; to Peter Clifton who walked the walls; to Sally Lasson, Peter Clifton, Colin and Gillian Clarke and Barbara Bunyan whose expertise at proof-reading and editorial skills were so appreciated.